Hermione Granger's Unofficial Life Lessons and Words of Wisdom

What Would Hermione (from the Harry Potter Series) Say?

Euphemia Pinkerton Noble

An Actionable Business Journal

E-mail: info@thinkaha.com
20660 Stevens Creek Blvd., Suite 210
Cupertino, CA 95014

Published by THiNKaha®
20660 Stevens Creek Blvd., Suite 210, Cupertino, CA 95014
http://thinkaha.com
E-mail: info@thinkaha.com

First Printing: September 2018
Hardcover ISBN: 978-1-61699-281-1   1-61699-281-6
Paperback ISBN: 978-1-61699-280-4   1-61699-280-8
eBook ISBN: 978-1-61699-279-8   1-61699-279-4
Place of Publication: Silicon Valley, California, USA
Paperback Library of Congress Number: 2018940361

Trademarks

All terms mentioned in this book that are known to be trademarks or service marks have been appropriately capitalized. Neither THiNKaha, nor any of its imprints, can attest to the accuracy of this information. Use of a term in this book should not be regarded as affecting the validity of any trademark or service mark.

Harry Potter is a registered trademark of Time Warner Entertainment Company.

This book is unofficial and unauthorized. It is not authorized, approved, licensed, or endorsed by J.K. Rowling, her publishers, or Time Warner Entertainment Company.

Warning and Disclaimer

Every effort has been made to make this book as complete and as accurate as possible. The information provided is on an "as is" basis. The author(s), publisher, and their agents assume no responsibility for errors or omissions. Nor do they assume liability or responsibility to any person or entity with respect to any loss or damages arising from the use of information contained herein.

Dedication

To my fellow Hermione-admirers,

May you find this book an inspiration as you journey through life. Remember what Hermione does when in doubt: "Go to the library." Or better yet, "Read this book."

How to Read a THiNKaha® Book

A Note from the Publisher

The AHAthat/THiNKaha series is the CliffsNotes of the 21st century. These books are contextual in nature. Although the actual words won't change, their meaning will every time you read one as your context will change. Be ready, you will experience your own AHA moments as you read the AHA messages™ in this book. They are designed to be stand-alone actionable messages that will help you think about a project you're working on, an event, a sales deal, a personal issue, etc. differently. As you read this book, please think about the following:

1. It should only take 15–20 minutes to read this book the first time out. When you're reading, write in the underlined area one to three action items that resonate with you.

2. Mark your calendar to re-read this book again in 30 days.

3. Repeat step #1 and mark one to three more AHA messages that resonate. They will most likely be different than the first time. BTW: this is also a great time to reflect on the AHAmessages that resonated with you during your last reading.

After reading a THiNKaha book, marking your AHA messages, re-reading it, and marking more AHA messages, you'll begin to see how these books contextually apply to you. AHAthat/THiNKaha books advocate for continuous, lifelong learning. They will help you transform your AHAs into actionable items with tangible results until you no longer have to say AHA to these moments—they'll become part of your daily practice as you continue to grow and learn.

Mitchell Levy, The AHA Guy at AHAthat
publisher@thinkaha.com

Contents

Foreword

As a Harry Potter tour guide, I have seen the way that Harry Potter affects the lives of thousands of people. From old to young, rich to poor, tall to short, Gryffindor to Slytherin, Harry Potter has a place in all of our hearts. Why? Because it matters. Because the story of Harry Potter, when we give it the opportunity, changes us. It makes us challenge our assumptions, question our morals, and value the things we often take for granted: love, friendship, and hope.

Walking around the ancient winding streets of Edinburgh, where the inspiration flew to Joanne Rowling in the 1990s like owls to the Great Hall in Hogwarts at breakfast, as she wrote the books that were to become our favorites, I'm reminded of the significance of her creation. Young children surround me as I walk and share knowledge, and I play a game with them.

"On the count of three, everybody shout out your favourite character!" I command. "Ready?"

"Yes!" A chorus of children responds.

"One… two… three!"

"HERMIONE!" "HARRY!" "SNAPE!" "HERMIONE!" "LUNA!" "HERMIONE!"

The young girls and boys who have all shouted Hermione look at each other, grins on their faces. There is a reason why they love this character so much. Obviously, many of the characters in Harry Potter have incredibly redeeming qualities and represent forces for good, but there's a reason that Hermione stands out.

Because Hermione starts as the underdog. She starts off as the geek, the nerd, the girl whose hair isn't done right and isn't very much fun and will follow the rules even though it's a lot more exciting to break them. And at the beginning, Harry and Ron even make fun of her for it, and then as the story goes on, they realize, as do we all, that without Hermione being exactly the way she is, Harry and Ron and the whole of the wizarding world would be completely lost.

Hermione represents hard work, cleverness, loyalty, friendship, and love. She holds the boys together, surprising them at every turn—whether it's through attending the Yule Ball with Victor Krum or erasing her parents' memories to keep them safe despite how hard it is for her. Hermione doesn't take the easy route, but she follows her instinct and follows her brain and takes whichever route she knows will have the best outcome. And that is why she is a role model for us all.

As a young witch, repeatedly referred to as a "Mudblood" by Malfoy, to rise to defeat the darkest of evils through nothing but her dedication and efforts, Hermione proves that we should never give up. She proves that with faith in yourself, your friends, and your community, anything is possible.

This book, *Hermione Granger's Unofficial Life Lessons and Words of Wisdom*, is a fun way to remind us of all these things. It allows us to imagine Hermione in situations we might find relatable, and to be able to follow her advice and continue to be inspired by her daily and in each situation that we face. We hope you enjoy the book, perhaps even as much as Hermione herself would have.

Olivia Kashti
Harry Potter tour guide who has shown thousands of tourists the inspiration that J.K. Rowling had for the Harry Potter series.

Share the AHA messages from this book socially by going to
http://aha.pub/HermioneSays.

Section I

Knowledge and Learning

Hermione Granger is called, "the brightest witch of her age," and for good reason. She loves to learn and expand her knowledge. At Hogwarts, she is always the first to raise her hand when the professor asks questions. Her impeccable interest in studying and willingness to learn as much as she can earned her that title.

Let Hermione teach you the best tips and tricks when it comes to studying. Apply these in your studies, and you're sure to get good grades. Remember that continuous learning will not only help you with your schoolwork, but it may also save your life and the lives of your loved ones someday.

1

Read "Hermione Granger's Unofficial Life Lessons and Words of Wisdom" at http://aha.pub/HermioneSays.

_____

_____

_____

2

Knowledge can save your life. Like the time Harry, Ron, and I were caught in the Devil's Snare! #WhatWouldHermioneSay

_____

_____

_____

3

When you're unsure about something, go to the library.
#WhatWouldHermioneSay

_____

_____

_____

4

After an exam, go through them thoroughly.
This gives you a chance to relearn.
#WhatWouldHermioneSay

_____

_____

_____

5

It's okay to be anxious for an exam. I
 believe that you won't perform
well if you don't feel a bit nervous!
#WhatWouldHermioneSay

_____

_____

_____

6

Don't cram. Create a study schedule
and follow it through. This better helps
you remember everything you learn.
#WhatWouldHermioneSay

_____

_____

_____

7

How to study effectively? Simple!
Study like you're the one who's going
to teach Potions class the next day.
#WhatWouldHermioneSay

_____

_____

_____

8

Learn with your heart. That's how I passed my OWL exams. #WhatWouldHermioneSay

_____

_____

_____

9

Learn how to say words right to communicate better. Remember, it's Wing-GAR-dium Levi-O-sa — make the "gar" nice and long! #WhatWouldHermioneSay

_____

_____

_____

10

Don't take your studies for granted. I truly believe that when you know better, you do better. #WhatWouldHermioneSay

_____

_____

_____

11

Remember that there's always room for improvement. Strive to improve. #WhatWouldHermioneSay

_____

_____

_____

12

Education opens new doors
for you to change the world.
#WhatWouldHermioneSay

_____

_____

_____

13

When it comes to knowledge,
don't stay the same — be better.
#WhatWouldHermioneSay

_____

_____

_____

14

Passing your OWLs takes passion for learning, hard work, and dedication. #WhatWouldHermioneSay

_____

_____

_____

15

If you want to improve the world around you, start by improving yourself. #WhatWouldHermioneSay

_____

_____

_____

16

You don't have to love studying to learn. You just need to like learning. #WhatWouldHermioneSay

_____

_____

_____

17

Respect teachers. They'll guide you through your whole time in school. I love Professor McGonagall. #WhatWouldHermioneSay

_____

_____

_____

18

Make reading books a hobby.
You never know when
you'll need the extra info.
#WhatWouldHermioneSay

_____

_____

_____

19

Develop a study habit that works for you
and stick to it. In time, you'll notice that
learning becomes easier and more fun.
#WhatWouldHermioneSay

_____

_____

_____

How to summon up your inner courage? Imagine that everything you want is on the other side of the mountain named "fear." #WhatWouldHermioneSay

http://aha.pub/HermioneSays

Share the AHA messages from this book socially by going to **http://aha.pub/HermioneSays**.

Section II

On Courage and Bravery

Whether you're a wizard or a Muggle, there are things in this world that can make us feel scared (aside from He-Who-Must-Not-Be-Named). Even those in Gryffindor, who are known to be brave, are afraid sometimes—including Hermione. We all have fears that we must face and conquer.

The first step toward conquering your fears is acknowledging the fear itself. It's not easy being brave, but as soon as you start, you become a shining star that everybody looks up to. Be brave despite knowing you can fail, and have the courage to continue when you do.

20

Being courageous doesn't mean that you don't fear anything. It means you can overcome it, no matter how big the fear is. #WhatWouldHermioneSay

_____

_____

_____

21

If you're afraid of the dark, turn on the lights. Don't let your fear leave you paralyzed. #WhatWouldHermioneSay

_____

_____

_____

22

Courage doesn't always pertain to fighting Voldemort. Sometimes, courage is failing an exam and saying, "I will try again tomorrow." #WhatWouldHermioneSay

_____

_____

_____

23

Saying the name of the person who scares you the most is the first step to overcoming your fear. Try saying Voldemort's name! #WhatWouldHermioneSay

_____

_____

_____

24

Do the things you fear. This helps you build up courage and overcome your fears. #WhatWouldHermioneSay

_____

_____

_____

25

Never let your fear of something bad happening stop you from doing something. #WhatWouldHermioneSay

_____

_____

_____

26

Think of fear as a friend. Fear points you
to the things you need to improve on.
#WhatWouldHermioneSay

_____

_____

_____

27

How to summon up your inner courage?
Imagine that everything you want is on the
other side of the mountain named "fear."
#WhatWouldHermioneSay

_____

_____

_____

28

Don't think that you can't overcome
your fears. You can and you will!
#WhatWouldHermioneSay

_____

_____

_____

29

Being brave doesn't mean you're not afraid. Being brave means you're the only one who knows you're afraid. #WhatWouldHermioneSay

_____

_____

_____

30

Standing up to our enemies takes a lot of courage, but standing up to our friends when needed takes a lot more. #WhatWouldHermioneSay

_____

_____

_____

31

Being courageous doesn't mean you don't fear anything, it means you know how to resist it. #WhatWouldHermioneSay

_____

_____

_____

32

Being afraid and choosing to be afraid are two very different things. Don't let fear stop you from doing amazing things. #WhatWouldHermioneSay

_____

_____

_____

33

If you want to stand out among others, you need to have courage. Courage shines! #WhatWouldHermioneSay

_____

_____

_____

34

Courage is being afraid and being fearless at the same time. Don't let fear take over your life. #WhatWouldHermioneSay

_____

_____

_____

35

Always remember that you're bound to do great things. A ship will always be safe on the shore, but that's not what it's built for. #WhatWouldHermioneSay

_____

_____

_____

36

When you make up your mind that you'll be successful, you're sure to succeed over your fears. #WhatWouldHermioneSay

_____

_____

_____

37

Bravery is admitting you're afraid of Voldemort and still choosing to take him on. #WhatWouldHermioneSay

_____

_____

_____

38

Bravery inspires bravery;
it's contagious.
#WhatWouldHermioneSay

_____

_____

_____

39

Be brave despite knowing you can fail,
and have the courage to continue
when you do. #WhatWouldHermioneSay

_____

_____

_____

At times of darkness, your family and friends will be your light. #WhatWouldHermioneSay

http://aha.pub/HermioneSays

Share the AHA messages from this book socially by going to
http://aha.pub/HermioneSays.

Section III

The Value of Friends and Family

Friends and family are certainly the best gifts we have ever received. They will always stand beside you, through thick and thin. You will always have their support, which is why it's important to keep them close. Hermione certainly feels this way about her friends, Harry and Ron.

No matter how far apart you are from each other, they will always be with you—in your heart.

40

Those who love us, our friends and family, they will never leave us, for they will stay forever in our hearts. #WhatWouldHermioneSay

_____

_____

_____

41

Friendship is like the sun:
beautiful and bright.
#WhatWouldHermioneSay

_____
_____
_____

42

Keep your friends close to your
heart so they're with you at all times.
#WhatWouldHermioneSay

_____
_____
_____

43

Harry and Ron are like the siblings
I never had. That's how deep our friendship
is. Do you have any friends like that?
#WhatWouldHermioneSay

_____

_____

_____

44

At times of darkness, your family
and friends will be your light.
#WhatWouldHermioneSay

_____

_____

_____

45

Even if you're up against a Bellatrix
Lestrange, your family will fight
beside you and help you win!
#WhatWouldHermioneSay

46

The Weasleys don't have much when
it comes to possessions; however,
together as a family, they're rich.
#WhatWouldHermioneSay

47

One is really lucky to have been loved deeply — you're safe and protected forever. #WhatWouldHermioneSay

_____

_____

_____

48

Home is where the heart is,
not where the Galleons are.
#WhatWouldHermioneSay

_____

_____

_____

49

Even though the world is against you, you
just need one friend by your side, and it'll
feel like you can do anything together.
#WhatWouldHermioneSay

_____

_____

_____

50

You can meet your best friends
anywhere, anytime — in my case,
I met them on the Hogwarts Express.
#WhatWouldHermioneSay

_____

_____

_____

51

You'll know you've found a good friend
when they know what you're going
through, even when you remain silent.
#WhatWouldHermioneSay

_____

_____

_____

52

Choose your friends wisely.
Don't let someone like
Peter Pettigrew sneak past you.
#WhatWouldHermioneSay

_____

_____

_____

53

Never be ashamed of your family,
even if you're Muggle-born.
#WhatWouldHermioneSay

_____

_____

_____

54

Harry and Ron can be quite crazy
sometimes, so it's my job to draw the line.
#WhatWouldHermioneSay

_____

_____

_____

55

A good friend will still understand
you despite your weaknesses —
they'll even help you out with them.
#WhatWouldHermioneSay

_____

_____

_____

56

Great friends protect
each other, like siblings.
#WhatWouldHermioneSay

_____

_____

_____

57

Your family will always love you,
no matter what. Remember to cherish
them. #WhatWouldHermioneSay

_____

_____

_____

58

Our family may not own everything,
but together, we have everything.
#WhatWouldHermioneSay

_____

_____

_____

59

At the end of the day, your family will
always be there waiting for you to come
home. #WhatWouldHermioneSay

_____

_____

_____

Be logical.
This helps you see even
the smallest of details that
everyone else misses.
#WhatWouldHermioneSay

http://aha.pub/HermioneSays

Share the AHA messages from this book socially by going to
http://aha.pub/HermioneSays.

Section IV

Overcoming Challenges

The road to success is filled with troubles and challenges. In order to overcome these, you should first be aware of how you view them. Some people view challenges as a bad thing, but Hermione knows that this can greatly affect how to handle them.

Challenges exist not to bring you down, but to pull you up. They exist for you to push past your limits and keep growing. Challenges, when overcome, bring great glory.

60

Challenges exist to make you stronger, so don't limit them. Instead, challenge your limits. #WhatWouldHermioneSay

_____

_____

_____

61

Be logical. This helps you see even the smallest of details that everyone else misses. #WhatWouldHermioneSay

_____

_____

_____

62

Go on an adventure, travel in the dark. Don't be afraid of the unknown. #WhatWouldHermioneSay

_____

_____

_____

63

The world we live in is full of suffering and challenges. Be the person who overcomes them. #WhatWouldHermioneSay

_____

_____

_____

64

A path with no obstacles doesn't lead anywhere. Where's your next obstacle? #WhatWouldHermioneSay

_____

_____

_____

65

When you see yourself running down a path and there's something blocking it, don't stop and turn around — keep going. #WhatWouldHermioneSay

_____

_____

_____

66

Life is dull without challenges. Overcoming challenges is what makes life exciting and worth living. #WhatWouldHermioneSay

_____

_____

_____

67

There's no room for growth if you live an easy life. If you want to grow, live fearlessly. #WhatWouldHermioneSay

_____

_____

_____

68

When facing challenges, know that
it can be hard and grueling. But also
remember that once you overcome them,
it's like the sun has just started to rise.
#WhatWouldHermioneSay

_____

_____

_____

69

One of the hardest challenges I faced was
overcoming my academics. Despite having
read all the books, I feared failing. I'm still
human, after all! #WhatWouldHermioneSay

_____

_____

_____

70

There will be times when everything seems to be falling apart. Don't let it get you down — rise above failure! #WhatWouldHermioneSay

_____

_____

_____

71

Those who dare to overcome challenges can achieve great things. #WhatWouldHermioneSay

_____

_____

_____

72

Challenges may break you, but if you overcome them, they will change you for the better. #WhatWouldHermioneSay

_____

_____

_____

73

Fear is what we have to be
fearful of. Conquer those fears!
#WhatWouldHermioneSay

_____

_____

_____

74

With challenges comes pain. Don't be
afraid of it, for it will become your strength.
#WhatWouldHermioneSay

_____

_____

_____

75

True challenges can be overcome; it's the imaginary challenges that can be unconquerable. Conquer from within. #WhatWouldHermioneSay

_____

_____

_____

76

Ron had a fear of spiders. But
when his friend was in danger,
he faced and conquered that fear.
#WhatWouldHermioneSay

_____

_____

_____

77

Always remember that you get to choose
what happens to you when challenges arise.
You can write your own story and choose
how it will end. #WhatWouldHermioneSay

_____

_____

_____

78

Your largest fear
is your greatest growth.
#WhatWouldHermioneSay

_____

_____

_____

79

There will always be a rainbow after the
rain. The bigger the obstacle you face, the
more glory you get when you overcome it.
#WhatWouldHermioneSay

_____

_____

_____

You will never really know how long you're gonna have to chase your dreams, so keep running and don't stop.
#WhatWouldHermioneSay

http://aha.pub/HermioneSays

Share the AHA messages from this book socially by going to
http://aha.pub/HermioneSays.

Section V

Chasing Dreams

Each of us has dreams we want to make into reality. Whether they're small (like passing your OWLs and NEWTs) or big (like becoming an Auror for the Ministry of Magic), dreams are something we should all be proud of.

On your way toward making your dreams come true, there will be people who will belittle them. This can be tiring, but don't let anything stop you. Be strong, be steadfast, and keep working until you've reached your goals and turned your dreams into reality.

80

Your dreams are your fuel. The more
you long for your dream to turn into
reality, the more you strive to achieve it.
#WhatWouldHermioneSay

_____

_____

_____

81

Don't dwell too much on your dreams.
Remember to live in the moment too!
#WhatWouldHermioneSay

_____

_____

_____

82

You have to be fearless in order to reach
your dreams. #WhatWouldHermioneSay

_____

_____

_____

83

Dream big, but remember to act on it or else it will stay a dream. #WhatWouldHermioneSay

---

84

I always dreamed about being a prefect. It wasn't easy, but all the hard work was worth it. #WhatWouldHermioneSay

---

85

Chase your dreams. Chase them until you're struggling for breath. Breathe, then keep on running. #WhatWouldHermioneSay

_____

_____

_____

86

Don't let others belittle your dreams. They're your dreams to begin with, not theirs. #WhatWouldHermioneSay

_____

_____

_____

87

When people start saying your dreams are unobtainable, you don't have to argue, just show them! #WhatWouldHermioneSay

_____

_____

_____

88

You will never really know how long
you're gonna have to chase your
dreams, so keep running and don't stop.
#WhatWouldHermioneSay

89

If your dreams are that important to
you, you'll still chase them even when
everything and everyone is against you.
#WhatWouldHermioneSay

90

Chasing your dreams can get
pretty tiring. Don't stop, just walk.
#WhatWouldHermioneSay

_____

_____

_____

91

Those who achieve their dreams
didn't quit, and those who didn't did.
#WhatWouldHermioneSay

_____

_____

_____

92

Never let anyone who gave up on their
dreams stop you from chasing yours.
#WhatWouldHermioneSay

_____

_____

_____

93

Keep working while other people are sleeping. Show your dedication to your dream. #WhatWouldHermioneSay

_____

_____

_____

94

The path to your dreams may be long and rough, but remember that anything worth reaching has the same path. #WhatWouldHermioneSay

_____

_____

_____

95

Dreams are for anyone, whether you're young or old. As long as you can breathe, you can dream. #WhatWouldHermioneSay

_____

_____

_____

96

Your dreams can come true as long
as you're willing to pursue them.
#WhatWouldHermioneSay

_____

_____

_____

97

Believe that you can make your
dreams come true. That's a start.
#WhatWouldHermioneSay

_____

_____

_____

98

Don't dwell on your
dreams — live them.
#WhatWouldHermioneSay

_____

_____

_____

99

Don't let your dream be just a
dream. Get up and make it happen!
#WhatWouldHermioneSay

_____

_____

_____

It's okay to think about life in the future, but don't think about it too much that you forget to live in the moment.
#WhatWouldHermioneSay

http://aha.pub/HermioneSays

Share the AHA messages from this book socially by going to
http://aha.pub/HermioneSays.

Section VI

Thoughts on Life

Knowing Hermione, she has many things running in her mind all the time. If you're one of the people who wonder what she's thinking, you're sure in for a treat.

Get to learn more about Hermione and what she thinks about life in general. Hermione will share useful words of wisdom that we can all live by to achieve true success and happiness.

100

Each one of us has got both light and dark inside; it's our actions that determine who we really are. #WhatWouldHermioneSay

_____

_____

_____

101

Someone who treats both their equals
and inferiors equally is a good person.
#WhatWouldHermioneSay

_____

_____

102

Despite differences in culture and language,
people can get along when their hearts are
one. #WhatWouldHermioneSay

_____

_____

_____

103

Whether you're a wizard or a muggle,
we're all human, and we're all worth saving.
#WhatWouldHermioneSay

_____

_____

_____

104

Always look for the happy things in life,
even when your surroundings get dark.
#WhatWouldHermioneSay

_____

_____

_____

105

Live with love inside your heart. If
you do, you're one of the lucky ones.
#WhatWouldHermioneSay

_____

_____

_____

106

Professor Snape was a great man. He risked
his life every day to protect the legacy of his
beloved. #WhatWouldHermioneSay

_____

_____

107

You control your life. You get
to choose how your story will
unfold. #WhatWouldHermioneSay

_____

_____

_____

108

We only get to live once, and that one
life should be lived to its fullest extent.
#WhatWouldHermioneSay

_____

_____

_____

109

Our lives are divided into chapters, like those in a book. Don't get down when everything doesn't work out, there's still another chapter! #WhatWouldHermioneSay

_____

_____

_____

110

When you've had a bad day, don't think
that tomorrow is going to be bad too.
Remember, it's only a bad day, not a bad life!
#WhatWouldHermioneSay

_____

_____

_____

111

As a Muggle-born witch, I was made fun of.
But I kept my chin high because I was proud
that I was both a Muggle-born and a witch.
#WhatWouldHermioneSay

_____

_____

_____

112

There will be hard and trying times,
but remember that life is worth living
and there will be lots of good times.
#WhatWouldHermioneSay

_____

_____

_____

113

A happy life doesn't always mean a rich life,
and a rich life doesn't always mean a happy
one. #WhatWouldHermioneSay

_____

_____

_____

114

Surround yourself with people
who see you for who you are and
still accept and value you.
#WhatWouldHermioneSay

_____

_____

_____

115

It's okay to think about life in the future,
but don't think about it too much
that you forget to live in the moment.
#WhatWouldHermioneSay

_____

_____

_____

116

Life is a one-time gift given to us,
so we better live it to the fullest.
#WhatWouldHermioneSay

_____

_____

_____

117

Remember to always look back and
appreciate everything you have and value
in your life. #WhatWouldHermioneSay

_____

_____

_____

118

If you keep your mind open, you are giving gifts all the time. Most of us just don't see them. You will, won't you? #WhatWouldHermioneSay

_____

_____

_____

119

Throughout life, whether good or bad—smile. It can brighten your day, as well as someone else's. #WhatWouldHermioneSay

_____

_____

_____

120

Life is meant to be lived. Go out there, meet new people, explore new places, experience new things, and do what you love to do. #WhatWouldHermioneSay

_____

_____

_____

Share the AHA messages from this book socially by going to
http://aha.pub/HermioneSays.

Section VII

Believing in Yourself

Hermione knows that the key to success is believing in yourself. No matter what your goals are and no matter what you want to achieve, you need to believe that you can achieve them.

Expect that not all people will support you; some will try to discourage you, and some will even try to mock your capabilities. You should be the first one to believe that you can achieve great things and work hard to reach your goals. If you don't believe in yourself, who will?

121

If you don't believe in yourself,
who will? #WhatWouldHermioneSay

122

Believe and you can.
That's the secret.
#WhatWouldHermioneSay

123

Our abilities are not the only things
that define us, but our choices do too.
#WhatWouldHermioneSay

_____

_____

_____

124

Don't be afraid to let people know who you truly are. Be yourself and be proud. #WhatWouldHermioneSay

_____

_____

_____

125

It's true that hard work is important, but what matters most is believing in yourself. #WhatWouldHermioneSay

_____

_____

_____

126

Your greatest competition is none other than yourself. #WhatWouldHermioneSay

_____

_____

_____

127

Stop comparing yourself to others and just believe in yourself! #WhatWouldHermioneSay

_____

_____

_____

128

Harry had a difficult time handling the darkness inside him, but in the end, he chose to believe in his true self and won. #WhatWouldHermioneSay

_____

_____

_____

129

The world will judge you based
on how you judge yourself.
#WhatWouldHermioneSay

_____

_____

_____

130

Believe in all that you are. Whatever
obstacle you face, there's something
inside of you that's greater.
#WhatWouldHermioneSay

_____

_____

_____

131

Believe that you're bigger
than any of your fears.
#WhatWouldHermioneSay

_____

_____

_____

132

Don't limit yourself,
always strive to be better.
#WhatWouldHermioneSay

_____

_____

_____

133

No one can make you feel down
if you don't let them.
#WhatWouldHermioneSay

_____

_____

_____

134

Have confidence that you're going to be successful. Believing in yourself is the key. #WhatWouldHermioneSay

_____

_____

_____

135

Believing in yourself when no one else does is brave and bold. #WhatWouldHermioneSay

_____

_____

_____

136

Don't worry about what anyone else thinks.
Worry about what you think of yourself.
#WhatWouldHermioneSay

_____

_____

_____

137

When people tell you that you can't, prove them wrong and say that you believe in yourself! #WhatWouldHermioneSay

_____

_____

_____

138

Have faith in yourself. Believe even if things are beyond the power of reason. #WhatWouldHermioneSay

_____

_____

_____

139

Believe that you're enough,
and let go of what the world says
you're supposed to be.
#WhatWouldHermioneSay

_____

_____

_____

140

Believing in yourself is just like magic.
When you do, you can make things happen.
#WhatWouldHermioneSay

_____

_____

_____

About the Author

Euphemia Pinkerton Noble

Inspired from the same cemetery in Edinburgh, Scotland, that Tom Riddle is buried in.

Other Books from Our Unofficial Harry Potter Series

The Unofficial Harry Potter Spellbook:
http://thinkaha.com/books/unofficial-harry-potter-spellbook

CPSIA information can be obtained
at www.ICGtesting.com
Printed in the USA
BVHW042025240920
589466BV00013B/719